Advanced Windows 7 Training Guide

A Training Course for Those
Who Want to Learn more about
using Windows version 7

By
Franklin Reid

Revised September 2013

Copyrights

Advanced Windows Training Guide - A Training Course for Those Who want to learn more about using Windows 7

Copyright Franklin Reid © 2013

Microsoft Office, Word, and Internet Explorer and their screen graphics are trademarks of Microsoft Corporation. Acrobat Reader is a trademark of Adobe Systems Incorporated.

About the Author:

Franklin Reid has been a technical writer for more than twenty years and has specialized in How-To books, producing many User Guides, Operation & Maintenance manuals, and software training manuals. He also is a passionate student of history and enjoys writing about it.

He has written articles on creating family history books, genealogy, photography, computer instructions, drafting, and other technical subjects. He is currently working on a historical book project. He lives in Ogden, Utah, with his wife and son.

He can be reached at his email:
Freid05@yahoo.com

By the same author

1. *Finding Zarahemla* – Available on Amazon.com

2. *Beginning Computers Training Guide* – Available on Amazon.com

3. *Advanced Windows XP Training Guide* – Available on Amazon.com

4. *Finding New Jerusalem* – Coming Soon

5. *Mormon Handcarts Going West – and East* – In work

6. *The Man Among the Gentiles* – In Work

Table of Contents

Author's Note

What I am describing in this study guide is Windows 7 on a standard desktop computer. It is the most common computer at home, at work, in the office, and in most schools. All of the instructions described here are for a desktop computer and may not be completely helpful for those with laptop computers. Desktop computers require a mouse and many, if not most of the instructions here, will require using the mouse.

Although laptop computers have a USB port and can be used with a mouse, if they are set up for it, but usually the keyboard has a rectangular area called a touchpad for this purpose. This touchpad includes two smaller areas near it which represent the keys of a mouse. This is usually below the typing keys but some makers have it set to the right. Users of laptops are very adept at using these extra keyboard tools to great efficiency.

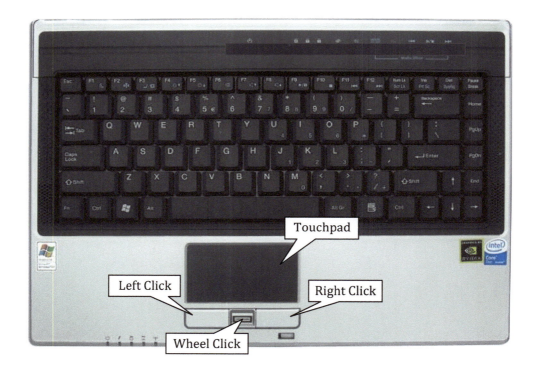

In my earlier work, *Advanced Windows XP Training Guide*, I tried to explain many of the hidden tools which can give you a greater understanding of the computer and your ability to control it. I used it to teach classes at the Ogden Regional Family History Center and many people liked knowing how to really get control of their computer. One told me, "It takes away the fear of the computer." I hope it will do the same for you.

Franklin Reid

Advanced Windows 7
A Six-Week Course

Introduction

The Microsoft Windows 7 operating system is a useful tool for getting our work done because it is the *master control program* under which we run all our other programs. We use it continuously while working on our various tasks with other programs as if the combination of the operating system (OS) and several programs, were one giant program. But many people under-use it or misunderstand its power. When we're in a program it's easy to think we are only using the tools which that program allows, not realizing that the program is using the tools Windows provides. For instance, we might be working in RootsMagic to do our genealogy and we use the different views to see, edit, and print our data thinking that we are only using the tools in RM when we are actually using the tools or hooks provided to the program by the operating system; in this case: Windows 7.

These hooks are called "system calls" because the program we are using at the moment calls on the computer system (Windows 7) for all of its handy and useful utilities. When programmers create a program, it is only necessary to create the tools specific to the work being done. For instance, a word processor needs to receive the characters typed on the keyboard and to present them on the screen. If you type an "r" you will see an "r" appear on the screen. But that process is actually using Windows system calls to get it from the keyboard, into RAM memory, and then onto the screen.

Because of its longevity, Windows has become a very powerful and stable place to work regardless of which of the many programs we are using. There are thousands of programs written for Windows 7 for use in every industry and endeavor known to us.

Although this is a six-week course, we can't teach you everything. But we will go over many methods, tips and tricks to help you get real control of your computer. It is hoped that it will take some of the mystery (and fear) out of your computer use. This training guide is designed for you to use at in a class or at home with your own computer. We hope it helps you in your personal computer work.

Part 1

Know Your Computer.

1. Using your mouse

Besides the keyboard, the most used item is the mouse.

What does "click" mean? -- It depends!

1. "*Click*" or "*select*" is <u>always</u> with the left button.
2. "*Double-click*" is <u>always</u> with the left button and is only used to open a file or a program icon.
3. "*Click-and-hold*" is <u>always</u> with the left button and is used for dragging an item from one location to another.
4. "*RIGHT-click*" is different. It is <u>always</u> with the *right* button but it only opens a small list or menu. This list will be different depending on where the cursor was when you right-clicked it.

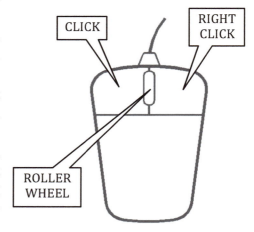

5. The wheel button is rolled to scroll through a document or up and down in a list. It functions much like the scroll bar.
6. You can also use the wheel as a button, to *click down* for scrolling, but it is only useful in some programs.

2. Understanding the desktop.

If Windows could think it would conclude that the desktop is just another window. It shows a large open area with program icons down the left side and a taskbar at the bottom. You can

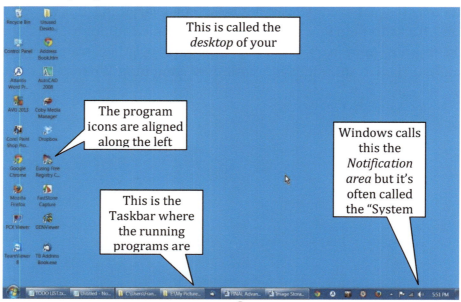

have it plain, of any color, or add a picture as a background.

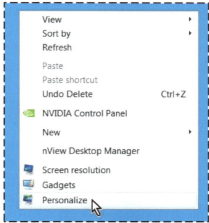

To change the background image or choose a solid color for the desktop, *right-click* anywhere in the open screen space and select *Personalize* at the bottom of the list. This will bring up a screen full of pictures in categories. To change the background, click on the image in the lower left corner titled "Desktop Background", below the box of other images.

Here you will change the background to any picture Windows 7 provides but also find any picture of your own which is stored on the computer. Don't forget to *Save* your changes to make them permanent.

Next, after clicking on *Desktop Background*, you will see another view of the images organized by category. If you move the slider bar down, to scroll down to the bottom, you will see the generic Windows 7 image which your computer had at first. These pictures are showing because the box above the images next to "Picture Location:" is showing the words: "Windows Desktop Background." If you click on the small triangle it will show a list of other choices.

Other choices include *Pictures Library, Top Rated Photos*, and *Solid Colors*. The ones shown

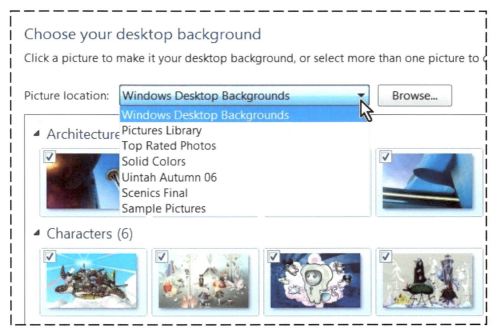

as *Uintah Autumn 06* and *Scenics Final* are my own photos found in those folders. Your own photos are accessible by using the Browse button and finding their folders. You can see that each image has a check mark in its corner. This means that they will be shown as a "slideshow" on a schedule. Below the pictures, there is text which says "Change picture every:" and a window where you can change the timing.

This is grayed out when only one picture is checked but will be available when two or more pictures are selected. Of course you can select the *Select All* button at the top to use all in that category or select individual pictures by holding down the control key to select them. To accept your settings click on Save Changes at the bottom then exit with the red X-button at the top right.

Returning to the desktop, you can see those small icons on the left and if you don't like their position you can easily move them anywhere you prefer on the screen. There is an invisible grid that keeps them straight unless it's been turned off. To drag an icon to a new place just *click-and-hold* on the icon, drag it to where you want it, then let go. To see what has been turned on or off, *right-click* in an empty area and again select *Personalize* at the bottom which we used a moment ago but this time you will select *View*. This will show a smaller menu with some of its items checked.

On my screen, for example, there are two items on the list that are checked. You can experiment with these, by clicking the checkbox to remove the mark, and return to the same menu to change it back. The desktop icons are showing on the screen only because that item is checked. If you uncheck it the icons will disappear. You may prefer to work that way. You can always turn them back on. If you check the *Auto arrange icons* the computer will decide where to put them – and there they will stay! Mine is turned off as you see.

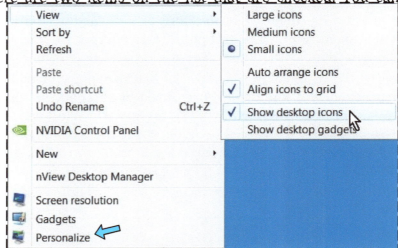

3. Using the Taskbar

As we saw above, the taskbar is the bar running along the bottom of the screen, set in its default location. To move it to another of the four sides first *right-click* an open area <u>on the taskbar</u> and remove the check mark from *Lock the Taskbar*.

You can now *click-and-hold* the taskbar, move it to the right edge of the screen, and let go. You can drag it to where you want it. It will attach itself to any of the four sides. Of course, you can drag it back to the bottom using the same steps. Don't forget to *lock the taskbar* by *right-clicking* on an empty place <u>on the bar</u> and select it. Later, we'll see an easier way to do this.

4. Adding programs to the Taskbar

In the old Windows XP you had a separate place on the taskbar called the Quick Launch area. When turned on you would see some program icons near the START button. In Windows-7 , this feature is built into the Taskbar itself. Click on the round START button or sphere, then find in this list the program you want on the taskbar, *right-click* it and select *Pin to Taskbar.*

Now you will see the small icon on the Taskbar. Once there, that program can be opened with a *single* click, no *double-click* required.

If you have too many icons on the Taskbar or want to remove one or more, just right-click on the icon in the *Taskbar* and select *Unpin this program from the Taskbar* on the menu and it will be sent back to the Start button list.

Another great feature of Windows 7 is that you can also create your own personalized toolbar that will sit near the right end of the taskbar.

Again, right-click on an empty area of the *Taskbar,* go up to *Toolbars*, then down to *New Toolbar* and click it. This will open the New Toolbar list which shows all the folders on your hard drive. Navigate to any folder you want and select it then click on the Select Folder button. Now you can see it near the right end of the Taskbar, the toolbar name you chose. You can see that I have selected the *My Family* folder.

If you Click on the small double-pointer symbol (>>) it will open that folder and show you the files and folders inside it. The folders are holders for more folders and show a small folder icon in front of the name. When you rest the cursor on a folder name, it will give you a list of the files and other folders *in that folder*. Put your cursor arrow on one of the folders and it will open to show more files. To open a file, click on a file (not a folder) and it will open up in the program which created it.

To remove that personal Toolbar, repeat the method you used to create it and *Click* on the name of the folder to remove the check and it will disappear from the Taskbar and return to the Start menu.

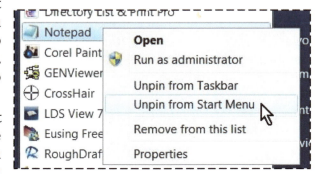

5. Using the right-click button

The purpose of the *right-click* button anywhere is to give you a short menu of choices. It will be a different menu or list depending on where you put the cursor arrow when you *right-clicked*. You have already seen the list when you *right-click* in an empty area of the screen. This was different than the menu when you *right-click* on the Toolbar.

If you place it on one of the desktop icons to the left it will be different yet. It is called *context sensitive* because it knows, and is sensitive to, where the cursor is set at the moment. If you place it in an empty area of the desktop and right-click, you will get one menu list. If you put the cursor on the *Taskbar*, or any icon, or on the *Start* button you will get different menu lists.

6. Using the Start button or Sphere

All the programs on your computer are found on the Start button list. Click normally on it and you will see a long list of programs that are installed on your computer. This is just another way to open a program. If you right-click the program you will get a short menu with some choices. If this program is not on the Taskbar you can change it here. You can also unpin it to the Start Menu or even Remove it from this list. This is where you can set it.

Either when you *click* normally and select it from the list or by *right-clicking* it. Now if you *right-click* on the *Start* button you get only two choices: *Properties* and *Open Windows Explorer*. The Windows Explorer will be explained later so we want to select *Properties* here.

But for now, let's *right-click* on the Start button and select *Properties*, then click on the *Taskbar* tab at the top. Now you will see a window with several choices. This tool gives you

12

six ways to alter the appearance of items on the Taskbar. Keep in mind that there are several ways to change the settings in Windows 7. On this screen you can. . .

1. Lock and unlock the taskbar, a different method than you saw earlier.
2. Automatically hide the taskbar from view – temporarily.
3. Use smaller icons instead of the standard size.
4. An easier way to relocate the taskbar to a different side of the screen
5. Group similar tasks together, and
6. Reduce the visible size of the System Tray or *Notification Area*.

For these same instructions, look near the bottom of this small screen with the *Taskbar* tab selected and you will see, in blue, the question: *"How do I customize the Taskbar?"* That will give you much of this same information. But for now, here are the six items listed above. Lets take them one at a time. Be sure you Click on the *Taskbar* tab at the top.

Because you <u>locked</u> the taskbar earlier, it is shown with the check mark there indicating it is locked. To unlock it here you can just click on the check and it will be unlocked. You'll notice that when you unlock the taskbar two things appear on it. They are a triple row of dots, hard to see, that are on the taskbar near the right end and another near the Start button.

These are indicators that the taskbar is unlocked but they are also used as a gripping place where you can *click and hold* your mouse and *drag* it sideways which changes the way the program tabs are shown. If you make any changes from this small window you will need to click on the *Apply* button to finish the job.

Now let's try the second item in the list of the Properties *Taskbar* tab to "hide" the Taskbar. Select the square to set it to <u>Auto-hide</u> the Taskbar, then click on [*Apply*]. You'll notice that the Taskbar disappears completely—but it is only temporary. If you move the cursor down and "bump" the bottom of the screen, the taskbar will reappear for your use. Move the cursor away and it "hides" itself again. This is useful if you need the taskbar out of the way, you can easily get to it when needed. If you set a setting don't forget to click the *Apply* button.

The next item on the Properties window is to change the location of the Taskbar. We saw earlier that with it unlocked you could drag it to another side of the screen. Now you can do it here and it's much easier.

The *"Taskbar location on the screen"* is showing: *"Bottom."* You can change it by pulling down the triangle and selecting a different place: *Left, Right*, and *Top*. Don't forget to click on the *Apply* button to make it happen.

Below this there is a *"Taskbar buttons"* which says *"Combine when taskbar is full."* This lets you combine into one tab, multiple files opened by the same program. They will load into a single space when the entire Taskbar is full. My Taskbar is not fully filled but when I open about fifteen or more they will "double up" on the tab. Looking at my Taskbar you will see that multiple files are open and shown on one tab.

When the setting is set this way, instead of seeing two or three instances of the program tab on the Taskbar they are combined into one. The program files behind can easily be shown by resting your cursor on the group of tabs. If you look closely you will see that there are more tabs, one behind the other. When you rest the cursor on a group of tabs it will open a thumbnail view of each file so you can select the one to click on to open at the moment. You can see this on the graphic. On this *Properties* window the other items below here can be discussed at another time.

7. Change Computer Shut Down Options

If you exited out of this window, *right-click* the Start button again and click on *Properties*. Now look at the top of this Properties window where you selected the *Taskbar* tab. Select the *Start Menu* tab. If it's not selected then click on it to see the settings.

The [*Customize*] button will be used later. The <u>Power button action</u> is basically choosing how you end your computer session. Whether set to Log Off, Restart, Shut Down or another method. To understand this it will help for you to briefly interrupt this instruction and reach down and *click* on the Start Button to show the list of programs. You will see the list of all the programs available to you. Now look at the bottom of this long list.

There, in the right panel, you will see a rectangle that probably says *Log off*, if it is set to that default. Clicking on the small pointer shows you there other choices for ending this session. You may notice that the **Log off**  words are not on this list as it is already set for this.

Changing it there won't change the default, it's intended for a one-time only purpose. For instance, sometimes you will need to turn the computer completely off or maybe you need to *Restart* the computer. You can make that change one-time here. Now let's return to the other window.

You can close it now by *right-clicking* again on the round Start button and select *Properties*. Under the *Start Menu* tab you can set this default, that is, the method you will see at the bottom of the Start button list each time you end your session, so you can just click on it.

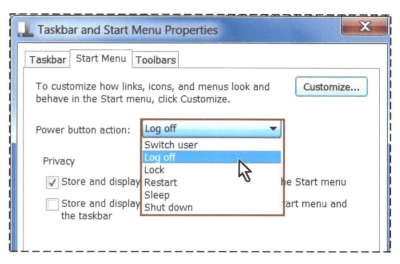

Now we will click on the small down arrow next to the setting beside "Power button action" and see the same list which now includes the *Log off* words. Some people prefer to [Shut down] the computer completely when finished with their work. This will turn off the electricity completely and the hard drive will wind down to a stop.

To restart it, you will need to push the ON/OFF button on the computer. Others will only [Log off] the computer. This terminates the Windows 7 system but keeps the computer running for next time of use. This window is where you can change the default. There is no advantage either way but if you are on a public computer, *Log Off* will still leave some of your information there for others to dig out. If you shut it down it flushes all caches and memories.

At home it's often best to just *Log Off* because the computer comes up much faster next time and with everything as you set it. Again, the bottom items in this window can be discussed later. Now let's click on the *Toolbars* tab. There you will see the checkmark in front of the *My Family* toolbar that we created earlier—the one now added onto the end of your Taskbar.

We learned earlier that the area called *the Notification Area* or *System Tray* is at the right end of the Taskbar. Since we are always

looking for more space for our program tabs, we have a way to help. Once again, in the *Properties* window of the Start button, and with the *Taskbar* tab selected, about half-way down we see *Notification Area* and a [*Customize*] button. When you click on this button you will see a large window with a list in the middle.

In the list are various ways in which you can alter the settings of icons in the Notification Area. But for now, we will leave this alone and look *below* this list where there is a small check box and the words, *"Always show all icons and notification on the taskbar"*. If it is checked, you will see all the program icons which have loaded themselves into this System Tray. This group might be large and will take up space on the Taskbar. The items shown here are all in my System Tray and as you can see they take up a lot of space. Here is how to shorten this group.

With this *Properties* window open and the Taskbar tab displayed, then click on the [Customize] button and at the bottom of the new screen, check the mark to clear it and watch

the System Tray area. It will reduce down to only two or three icons. Where are the others? If you will put your cursor on the small triangle which now is there, pointing up it will say, *"Show Hidden Icons"* , and if you click on it you will see a little window with the other items shown. Just so you know that they are still available if needed but not taking up space on the Taskbar. If you click on the Customize word it will open this same larger window where you changed it. Now you can close the Properties window.

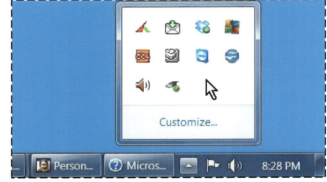

8. Changing the clock settings

One more thing to show on the Taskbar at the very end is the clock which shows the time in digital format. Set your cursor on the numbers and it will show the dateIf you want to change the time or the day and date too. If you *click once* on the numbers showing the time to open a window.

There you will see an analog (round) clock and a calendar showing the current time and date. Under it is the note: "Change date and time settings." Click on these words and it will open a larger screen to do just that. With this you can select the [Change date and time...] button. Then you

will see a similar window for actually changing the time and date.

This will open the Date and Time window. Now, select the *"Change date and time..."* words. This will open the window to "Set the date and time". Again, you can see the calendar and clock but here you can change them both. To change the calendar just click on a date in the calendar. When you exit this will be the new date showing at the end of the Taskbar.

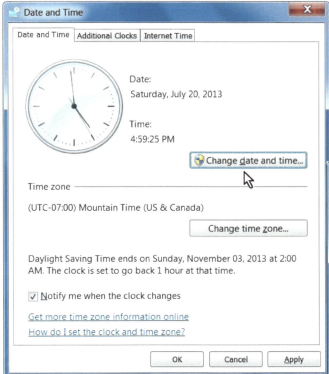

To set the time in this same window click on the digital time below the round clock. Click on the hour space and then click on the small arrows, up and down, to make the change. You will notice that the hands of the clock will move accordingly. Repeat this for the minutes and the minute hand will move. The same for the seconds. OK to finish.

You can also see a [Change time zone] button. Click on it to show a small *Time Zone Settings* window. Pull down the Time Zone pointer and it will show all the time zones in the world. The Zero point is shown in Dublin, Edinburgh, Lisbon, and London. Click on this if you are in this time zone.

I am in Utah USA so my time is Mountain Time. All times zones west from Zero are minus (-) one hour. Those to the east are plus (+) one hour. Thus mine here is minus seven hours. Also, below that setting you can set the Daylight Saving Time for your area. Many countries don't use this, and even Arizona here doesn't use it. Be sure to [OK] your changes or if you want to leave it as-is click on [Cancel].

9. Clearing the Desktop.

Sometimes you want to minimize all windows with one click so you can see the background picture or other icons on the desktop. You do this

with the tiny rectangle at the right end of the Taskbar. It's nearly invisible but if you can click on it the screen will clear of all programs. They are not closed, but just have been minimized to their respective tabs on the Taskbar. Now only the icons are showing on the background. Click it again to reverse this process. If you open a program while in this state then the "click again" won't work. Just open the programs you need in the normal way by clicking on its tab on the Taskbar.

10. Minimize and Maximize the Window

We are all familiar with the three buttons in the upper right corner of each Window. You can use this to *Minimize, Maximize,* and *Close* the Window using these corner buttons. We commonly click on the red button to close the program. We can also Minimize the current program window and send it to the bottom tab on the Taskbar where it's available for use when needed.

If you have all your windows set to the Maximum they will look like the upper view in our example which shows not one square but two, meaning you can unlock the window from all sides and reduce its size smaller. This means if you click it the window will unlock from the sides and will be set in a smaller unlocked mode, neither 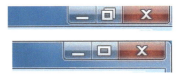 Maximized or Minimized to the Taskbar. In the lower view, there is just a single square, indicating that if you click it the window will expand to Maximum and lock itself to the edges. In this condition, the window can't be moved or resized because it is locked.

If you unlock the window and make it only a little smaller than full screen, you can then Maximize the Window again by clicking on the same button. Also, if you *double-click* anywhere on the top bar of any window it will do the same thing; *double-click* again to reverse it.

11. Ending or exiting a program

You already know that you can exit and close any program by clicking on the red X-button. There are actually four ways to close a window or program.

First, you can click on the red button. If you have not saved your file in that program it will prompt you to do so.

Second, we can go down to the taskbar and find the tab for the program, *right-click* on it then select *"Close window"*.

Third, you can type **Alt+F4** on the keyboard and the program you are currently in will close. If you have done some work there, it will first ask you if you want to save the changes. Your choices are [Yes], [No], and [Cancel].

Fourth, you can pull down the **File** menu for that program and select *Exit* at the bottom of the list.

Part 2

RAM memory, Hard Drive Storage, and the Windows Explorer

1. When is a computer like a school classroom?

In this cartoon we can see the teacher sitting at her desk. She takes file folders out of the storage cabinet (hard drive) and puts them on the desktop. From this she can sort out the various subjects and find the one she wants. Maybe it will be math problems which she writes on the board (RAM). The board functions as a short term memory to hold the problems for the students. At the end of class, she erases the board, gathers the folders on the desktop and stores them in the file cabinet.

This is exactly what we do with our computers. We turn on the computer, then from the

hard drive we open a file by double-clicking on it which puts it into RAM and the program that created it opens before us. We can see the file and go to work to make changes as needed. When we are finished, we close the program and save the file on the hard drive storage. This process also erases the program from RAM.

Each of these places where data exists: the file cabinet, the desk, and the blackboard represent the same things in a computer. In the computer they are the storage on the hard drive (the file cabinet), the desktop with a folder and several sheets, and the blackboard (the RAM). Why is the blackboard like the computer RAM? Because it has a very short duration. When the teacher finishes with the math lesson she can erase it. As long as it was on the board it was a form of storage to remember what was said but once erased, it's gone. When we save and close the computer program the image on the screen is gone.

As we saw in Part 1, there are many tools within Microsoft Windows 7 to allow us to customize our screens to our own way of working. This time we will learn more of these customization tricks. But first we must consider the computer's inner workings.

2. What is RAM and what is the hard drive for?

On our computer screens we have a desktop on which are several programs running. These only show one sheet at a time, just like the teachers desk. But to get them there you had to go to the storage, (the hard drive) and find the right file and open it on the desktop.

As mentioned above, the RAM is like the blackboard and is only used as a temporary place to show information while the computer (or the class) is running. When the class is over the teacher puts away the files into the file cabinet and erases the blackboard. In this same way, when you are finished doing some work on the computer you save the work onto the hard drive, clean off the desktop by closing down the program and logging off or shutting down the computer.

RAM is like the teacher's blackboard – it is the *working place* for the computer to do its work. The teacher will write an English diagramming lesson or some math problems. A large blackboard gives more space to work and many school classrooms have very long blackboards across the front. This gives a large place to work. Maybe, she will be showing a history lesson in one part, having students writing on the board at another and still have the test at the other end covered with the map.

Our computer's RAM memory is the same way. More RAM space means more work can be done and done faster. Imagine a teacher using a very small blackboard, say 2 x 3 feet. If she wants to teach anything she must be constantly erasing to make space for the next part. This slows down the process greatly. A larger RAM, like the larger blackboard, makes everything work faster and more efficiently. This is regardless of the amount of storage space on the hard drive.

Some people confuse the RAM with the hard drive storage space. They will say that their computer is slowing down so they decide to delete some programs off the hard drive. This would be like the teacher emptying two of her four-drawer file cabinet in the hopes that it will make the blackboard larger. But we know that these two items are not related and so it makes no difference to the RAM to delete files off the hard drive any more than throwing files out of the file cabinet would give the teacher more blackboard space. One is for storage and the other is for current work.

A RAM module which is plugged into a long slot in the computer box.

Older style hard drive which installs inside the computer box.

This photo shows an older style hard drive (but very similar to the newer ones) on the left, and a RAM module on the right. The RAM has a long connector of brass contacts which plugs into a long slot on the main circuit board of the computer. These are two basic components of every computer. If you need more storage space you—or a technician—will replace this hard drive with another which looks very similar but because of newer technology it will hold a much more data in its storage space.

If the computer needs more working room (RAM) the technician can replace the older lower capacity RAM module with a newer one with more RAM available. It would be like the school deciding that the teachers need more space to teach from and replace older smaller blackboards with much larger ones.

Older computers could easily function with 128 kilobytes (kb) of RAM but when they were later replaced with modules which held eight-times this or 1000 kilobytes which is 1 megabyte (MB) of RAM it made them work much faster. Today there are computers with larger RAM yet. The computer I am writing this on has 4 megabytes (MB) of RAM but there are many now which have eight or more MB of RAM.

Hard drives have gone from 128 Kilobytes of storage to a 1Megabyte (MB), to 500MB, to 1000MB which is 1 terabyte (TB). Technology marches on and the computers must keep up with ever larger software programs that require more storage and more RAM for faster speed.

Now we understand that RAM is a temporary place in which all the work is done. The Hard drive is a storage place where all the things installed on your computer are stored. This is not temporary but permanent. It remains there next time you turn on the computer. In the next section we will discuss all the components on the hard drive.

3. Folders and Files – what's the difference?

Before we look at the file manager in Windows 7 we need to explain the difference between files and folders in the computer. They are like an office file cabinet which holds many folders organized into categories. There would be folders in one area called *EMPLOYEES*, another called *SALES* and yet another called *TAXES*. If we take out one of these folders and open it we will find papers which describe some part of the folders. For instance, the sales folder would include paper files with the names of customers and the amount they had purchased.

If we look at this as a list it would show that the folders would show each part of the files it contains. Here is a possible example:

BIG MANUFACTURING COMPANY
EMPLOYEES
    Office Staff
    Manufacturing Staff
    Maintenance Staff
SALES
    Monthly sales report
    Customer Orders
    Accounting reports on total sales.
TAXES
    IRS Forms

Last Years Taxes

Quarterly Taxes Paid

In our Big Manufacturing Company (BMC) example, we see the top folder with the company name, followed by three folder categories, *Employees, Sales,* and *Taxes.* Then in each of them are other categories which have individual documents in them. These categories can be typed directly in as names for folders and files. The Big Manufacturing Company couldn't function if it had many file cabinets and papers just stuffed anywhere convenient at the moment. They wouldn't be able to find any of their files. Remember, a file represents the piece of paper you look at on the screen and the folder is where it is stored. To do this we need to open the Windows file manager, called *Explorer.*

4. Opening The File Manager

The computer can store a great deal of information and if we don't have some system to control it we can easily get lost. It would be like a public library with thousands of books which are on any shelf anywhere without regard to author or subject matter. Imagine going to such a library and trying to find the right book by simply walking along the aisles and reading every title. You would potentially have to read all the titles in the library to find the book you want. Thankfully, a man named Melvil Dewey invented a system in 1873 to fix this problem. It is the Dewey Decimal System which is in use in all libraries around the world.

Every text book needs a table of contents and an index. Also, every computer needs some way to see the entire contents of the hard drive. This storage space is organized, as mentioned above, into folders, sub-folders, and individual files. When you create a file of information such as a genealogy record, a business record, or even your favorite music, it is placed into a folder – somewhere on the hard drive. But where and in what order? Our next step is to open the Windows 7 file manager.

Windows 7, like the many versions before it, has a very good file manager built into the system. It is called the *Windows Explorer* because it lets you explore all the windows on the

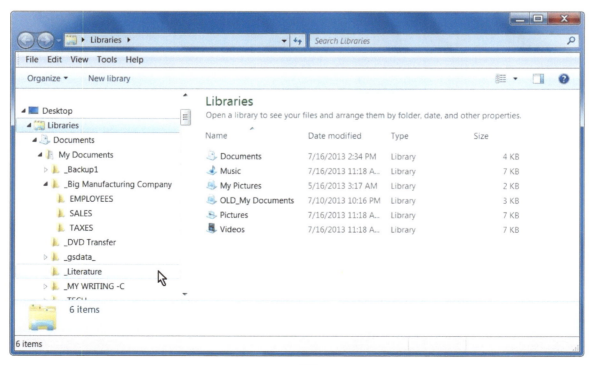

computer. This is **not** the *Internet Explorer* which is a browser used to browse the Internet. The internal file manager is often called simply, *Explorer*. To find it you only need to *right-click* on the Start sphere again, like before, but this time click on "Open Windows Explorer."

When it opens, you can see that it displays the computer's drives and main folders in the left panel and the folders, sub-folders, and files on the right. It has many built-in tools for copying, moving or deleting files, as well as creating new folders as needed. Looking closer, we see that Libraries is selected on the left. This view shows Libraries in three places. At the top, on the left and the heading on the right.

The Libraries group is made up of groups of other subjects, such as Documents, Music, Pictures, and Videos. You can later learn to add more to this. We will mostly be using the group called Documents. Within it are all the documents which have been stored on the computer. This could be your genealogy documents, your writing, your finances, your email messages, and anything else you want to put here. We will learn how to do this in Part 3 but for now we need to show one more thing. Don't close the Explorer window now as it will be needed.

The great thing about Windows 7, like it's former versions, is that it has these windows which act like separate computers on the same machine. What this means is that the Windows Operating System (OS) was created to have many independent places, like separate computers, all running simultaneously within your computer. Unlike the old DOS days where the system could only hold one program at a time in RAM and on the screen, Windows allows many separate ones to be running at the same time.

That's the beauty of it, you don't need to close one program to open another. You could have several (even dozens of) programs running at the same time. Each of them is represented by a tab on the taskbar at the bottom of the screen. How does the computer know which one you are using at the moment? Easy, it is the one that is in front.

The *copy and paste* tools are great for transferring data from one document to another. We can also copy an entire document or a sub-folder from one folder and paste it into another. In Part 3 we will learn how to do this.

Part 3.

Using the Explorer

1. Learning to Navigate with the Explorer

To navigate means to use the Explorer window to look around your computer and to move from one folder to another to find files. To start, bring up the Explorer and look at the folders on the left panel. Notice that there are tiny triangles in front of each item listed. If you don't see them it is because they turn off when the cursor is on the Right side. Move it to the left and they will turn on. If some folders still don't have a symbol then there are no more folders in that one, only files.

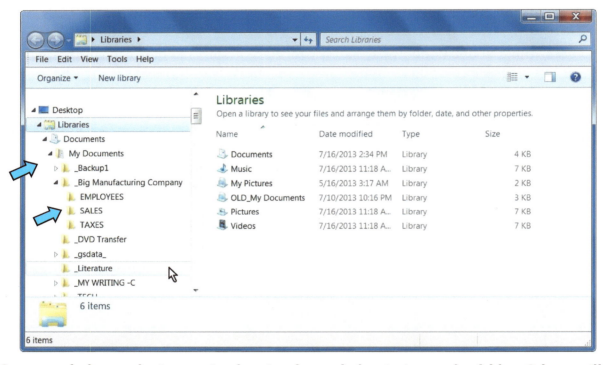

Some symbols may be just a simple triangle symbol pointing at the folder. Others will be solid black and pointing downward to indicate the folders below. These indicate whether that folder is currently open or closed. If you click on the triangle it will change to the other state; it represents what you can see if you click on it. When it is an open symbol it means you can open it by clicking. Then solid black shows the folders below it are what is inside. It's in an indented our outline form. As you keep clicking on the symbols they will turn black and open to show the contents below.

2. Learning to use Explorer.

Now that we have found the Explorer utility and have learned how to open it, we can use it to find, arrange, move, and delete our folders and files and to organize our work to our own liking. The Explorer gives us full control over all the things in or connected to our computer. We can even look at the folders and files in other drives besides the built-in hard drive. We can look at the files in an external drive, a disk, a USB flash drive and the files related to our printers and modems. We can look anywhere in the computer. Now we'll learn some basics. For instance, we can...

- Use the Explorer to organize information into folders and files.
- Turn on or off the file type or extension on each file.
- Start a file in its own program.
- Using the Search tools.
- Find lost files with the Search tool.

3. Use the Explorer to Organize folders and files

To understand how the computers organizes or orders all the data it has we have to keep in mind that the folders and files in each list are always arranged in ASCII *order*. You know it as *alphabetical* order, but with some additional powers to accommodate other symbols not in our standard alphabet. The first step used by the computer to *order* your folders and files is to look at the first character in the name.

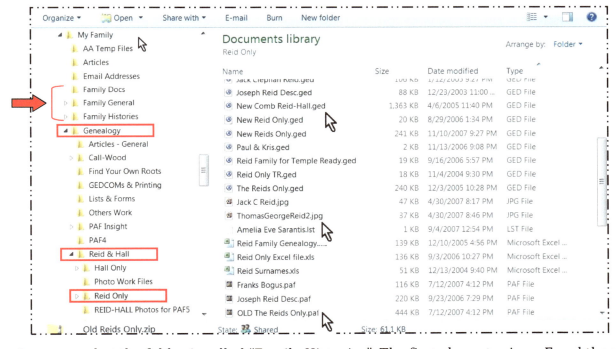

Let us say that the folder is called "Family Histories". The first character is an F and the next is an A and so on. This will continue to find the correct place for this name. If the first word is "Family" then all the folders with this as the first word will be together. Then it will look at the second word, again looking at the characters—first to last. This second word will determine the order in the list.

Now, looking again at a portion of the Explorer on my computer, you can see that *Family Docs* is followed by *Family General*, then by *Family Histories*. In order, they all have *Family* but one has the first letter of the second word as D, G, and H. After that, is the *Genealogy* folder, because *G* follows *F*. It's really quite alphabetical.

4. Turn on or off the file type or extension on each file

Now we see on the left side as I have selected, under <u>*Genealogy*</u>, the *Reid Only* folder. You can see I have broken down the information into smaller categorized groups. In this last folder, you can see all my files there on the right. What you want to look for now is the different endings on the file names. Each file name on the right is followed by a dot (.) then three more letters. This is called the *File Type* or file *Extension*.

If you don't see this extension on the filenames it's because it has been turned off. To turn it on go to the top menu line of *Explorer* and click on *Tools*, then *Folder Options*, then the *View* tab. Going down this list you will see an item that says:

[ ] Hide extensions for known file types

If there is a check mark there, click to remove it so it *won't hide* the file extensions. Click on *Apply* then *OK* to complete the action. After a moment, your filenames should have an extension on each one. Some are listed here:

- .paf   This is a file that can only be opened by the PAF5 or other genealogy program.

- .jpg   Pronounced "Jay-Peg" and indicates it is a picture or photo and can be opened by that type of program.

- .xls   A file opened by Microsoft Excel or other *spreadsheet* program.

- .ged   A file created by PAF5 called a GEDCOM file and can be shared with others and then imported later on another computer.

- .txt   A text file opened by the Notepad program but can also be opened by any word processor. We often keep family notes in it.

- .exe   This is an *executable* file, which means it's a program. If you could see the folder where PAF5 is located, it would have this extension. Also, this Explorer program we are using, is listed elsewhere as Explorer.exe. An .exe file is like an icon on the main desktop screen; you can just *double-click* on it and it will open. More on this later.

There are many other File Types and it is good to learn the ones that you will use the most. You can look for files by their file type extensions. One of the most common problems with files is they get lost. People don't know where to find them, when created. This Explorer allows you a way to find them by using the Search tools.

Having learned all this, let's also learn how to arrange the files differently. One of the easiest ways is to simply rename the file. If you rename the file from "Zanzibar" to "A Trip to Zanzibar", the file would move from the end of the list to the top. The first letter being A where it was Z. If your files are named like this:

History and Geography – Zanzibar

Photos – Zanzibar

Trip and Hotel – Zanzibar

The files would be located in their respective alphabetical order. But if you renamed them to this:

Zanzibar – History and Geography

Zanzibar – Photos

Zanzibar – Trip and Hotel

This will group them all together in your list. This is true of the list of files and the list of folders. This would be a good time to create a folder called Zanzibar and put these files into it. Keeps them in there place.

5. Start a file in its own program

Sometimes you may wish to search for a file then open it directly without first opening its creating program. For instance, you may have a family history file which you have found and you can tell from its extension that it is a .doc file which means it is a document file that can be opened with Microsoft Word or some other word processor. You could, of course, find that program on your list of programs from the Start button, open it then go looking for the file again to bring it up for editing. But since you are already there in the Explorer and can see the folder you want, you have two options.

First, you can *right-click* the file and select "Open" from the top of the context menu. Another way is to simple *double-click* on the file itself. It will find its creating program and open it there ready for your editing.

6. Using the Search tool

With the Explorer up on the screen we can do some searching for a file. I do this whenever I can't locate it. Let's suppose that I want to find my companies list of employees in the Big Manufacturing Company (BMCo) folders called *Office Staff*. I've looked in the EMPLOYEES folder and it's not there. I thought it was but its not and now I'll have to do a search for it.

At the top of the Explorer window, we see two long bars. One shows the location where I am currently viewing files: (>Libraries > Documents > My Documents >). To the right of that is a bar which has the grey words, "*Search My Documents.*" This will reflect whichever folder you have selected in the left column. If I had selected General Files, it would say *Search General Files.* Now if we *normal-click* on this bar it will bring down another context menu. But first let me explain:

If we just type in a search word such as *Office* or *Staff*, it will search in all folders and

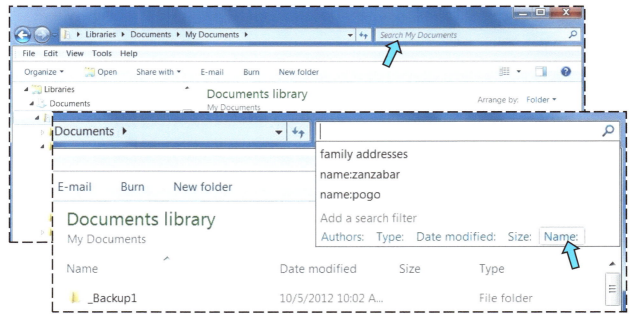

subfolders below this point and you may get a very long list. This is sometimes necessary but not this time. We know the name of the file is *Office Staff* but we can't find it. Notice along the bottom of this context menu is a list of word choices to aid your search.

If you select the word *Name:* it will place it in the top bar and then when you type the search folder *name* it will begin searching. To the left of this, you may see a green moving bar which indicates it is indexing the folders for a future faster search. When you have done this once, the green bar usually doesn't occur.

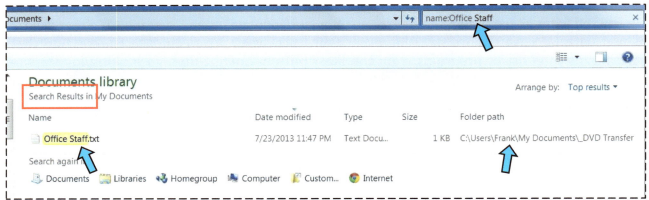

When it's finished searching it will show a "Search Results" list which shows the title you gave it to search on in ==yellow==. Over to the right is the location where it was found. Now you know where to go get it. You can, of course, just double click on the yellow title and it will open for you.

7. Find lost files with the Search tool

If we take those same steps and select the Name: tool it will only search for our word in the

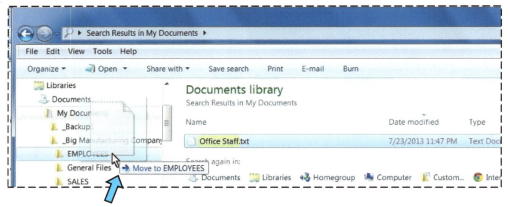

names of the files, not inside the files. So you can see that I have selected name and then typed the two words I am looking for. It looks like this: name:Office Staff.

As you can see, the Explorer Search tool found the missing file as it is listed in the window in yellow. If you look to the right under *Folder path,* you will see the entire path leading to that file. It shows that is located in the **C\:Users\Frank\My Documents_DVD Transfer** folder (Hmmm. What is it doing there? This is how easy it is to lose things) In any case, we can now use the left side of the Explorer to find the folder it should be in and move the file to where it belongs.

To move it, locate the correct folder on the left, in this case it is EMPLOYEES, then on the right put your cursor on the *Office Staff.txt* file and *click and hold* the left mouse button and while holding down, drag the file to the left and when it is on the correct folder, you get a reminder of what you are doing. There is a difference between Move and Copy. Then let go.

In the process, you will see a graphic image of a document and the message *Move to EMPLOYEES* showing in the left. If you decide you want to retain a copy where it was, then you can press the Ctrl key, while still holding the mouse key down, and the word *Move* will change to *Copy*. Now the file will be either *moved* or *copied* depending on which you chose to do. It will happen when you release the mouse button. You will use this *copy-paste* tool often as you become more advanced in using the Explorer.

I mentioned earlier that if you *don't* use the Name:*filename* for searching it may give you a long list. Sometimes this is preferred. The advantage to using a search based on the name, as mentioned, is a shorter list and lets you find the file because you know the file's name. But what if you can't remember it? What if all you remember is some words inside the file? If I know it's a family history file but can't remember the name but I do know it is about a handcart company I can search on "handcart" to find all the files with that word in the file.

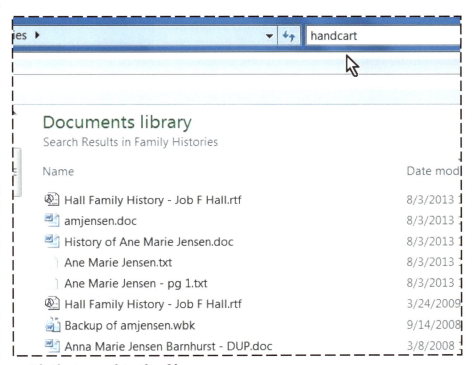

This list is longer but it shows all the file names with the word "handcart" somewhere in the file. At the bottom left of that screen it tells me there are 54 files that meet this criterion. Now I can look down the list and try to remember which file it is that I wanted to open. This becomes a great tool for finding lost files or files that we have used before but can't remember the name. This is why the Windows Explorer is so important to understanding and controlling your computer and its files.

8. Avoiding lost files

There is a way to avoid losing your files in the first place. We all have done this: we *Save* a file and then later we can't find it. Where is it? Why did it go somewhere else? To answer these questions we need to go to a program, any program, and see where it is *set to save its files*, as its default. Each program does it differently. This method is not done in Explorer or even in Windows 7, but is done in your working program. It only works for a program that produces your own work files, such as a word processor or your genealogy program. I will use PAF as an example. This is not a PAF training guide so I will only show the steps to do this so you can see how it's done in many other programs.

Open the PAF5 (or other) program that holds your genealogy data. Once up on the screen you have access to the list of pull-down menus at the top. Pull down the *Tools* menu and select *Preferences* at the bottom. In the Preferences window, select the *Folders* tab at the top.

This will show you a list of folders where you can place these five types of files. The top one is *PAF Files* which means the files created by you as you create and edit your genealogy records. If this is blank, here is where you will tell PAF where to put the file as a default. In the graphic image, you can see three arrows. They are pointing to the things I have chosen. To make this change, first click on the *Folders* tab, then the small button with three dots [...] which is to the right of the *PAF Files* line. This opens a search window so you can go to the folder where you want your genealogy data to go <u>every time</u> PAF saves the file. Select the folders needed.

You can see that I have gone down to the folders *Genealogy > Reid-Hall folder*. Select the folder then click on OK. This will automatically add the full path to this window. Then click OK to save it. The purpose of this is to have a definite and default location where all files of a type are stored on your computer.

You will need to do this on YOUR OWN COMPUTER as it won't work when you do this on another computer then take your data home. It is a setting on *that computer*, not in your file. It's a good idea, if you are on another computer, to check here first to see where the program on *this computer* is placing your files. It isn't necessary to change it but is enough just to see where it's putting the files. In some programs if you click anywhere in that field, then tap the [End] key on your keyboard, it will move the cursor to the end of the path line so you can see the folder the data is stored in.

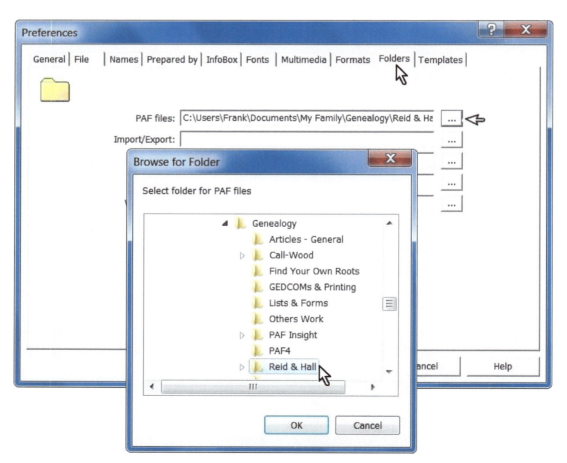

Part 4

Organizing your work by creating folders

1. Use the Explorer to add personal folders to the computer.

Let's create a fresh folder for our data. First, find the higher-level folder you want to put it under. This might be you're *My Family* folder and you want to put a *Vacation* folder into it. Select the folder on the left. Now, you will see how to create a new folder on the left side. I have selected the *My Family* folder and want to put a folder under that called "Vacation 2013."

Put your cursor on the *My Family* folder name and right-click to bring up a context menu. Near the bottom put your cursor on the word "New" just over to the right click on "Folder." You will see a "New Folder" open in the left side ready for you to type in the name, "Vacation

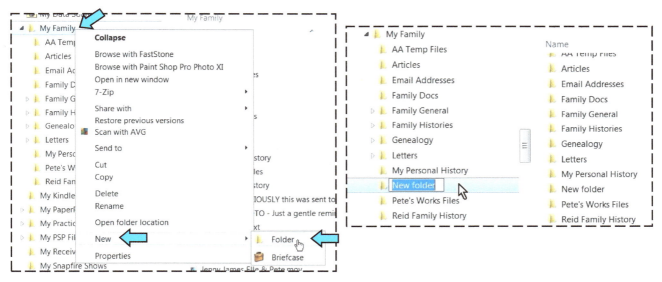

2013."

Now set your cursor on this new folder and *right-click* again. This will bring up the same context window. Select *New* again then *Folder*. Now you can type in the first folder here, "Zanzibar History and Geography." Now just repeat the process for each folder name. Once finished, you can now add in the files needed in each folder.

2. How To Rename Your Folders And Files

Looking at my folders I see I have a problem. In this graphic, under Vacation 2013, I created sub-folders for each of the categories but if you look close you will see I misspelled the one for photos. It's "Zaznibar" and it should be "Zanzibar." Let's see if we can fix it. Place your cursor on that misspelled folder and right-click. Again you will get the context menu as you did before. Near the bottom is the *New* command we used earlier but higher up from there is the *Rename* command.

When you select this instead of opening a [New Folder] in your list to type a name, it opens the folder the cursor was on, ready for editing. Now you can either retype it or just correct the letters as you wish. That done, it's now correct in both sides.

As you can see in this graphic I found the folder with the misspelled word. Then I right-clicked on it and when the context menu came up as before, instead of clicking on *New* I clicked on *Rename*.

This caused the folder name to take on a different look and opened the name for editing. Then I corrected the name and hit the Enter key. This finalized the process and the corrected name shows in the list. This will show it corrected everywhere because Windows uses this list for its look-up place.

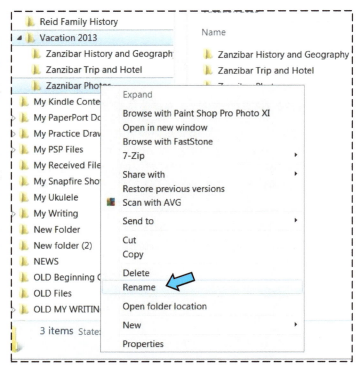

3. Changing the view of your files

Let's look at a couple of features more while we are here. As you look at your files on the right side, you can see that the information for each one is in a column. At the top of each column is a header. The first is the *Name*, then *Date Modified*, *Size*, and *Type*. This view shows the *details* of the file. If you prefer to see the details in a different order, say the Size column closer to the Name, it's easy to change. Just place your cursor on the header name, hold down the mouse button and drag that header left or right to a different location then release the button.

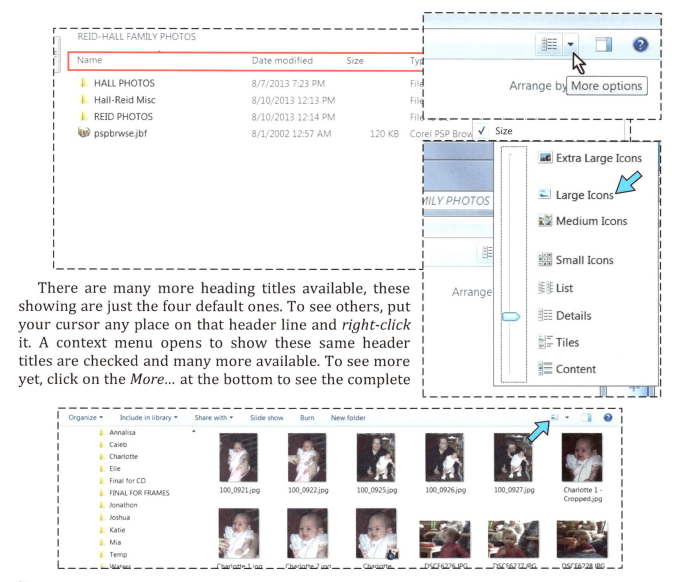

There are many more heading titles available, these showing are just the four default ones. To see others, put your cursor any place on that header line and *right-click* it. A context menu opens to show these same header titles are checked and many more available. To see more yet, click on the *More...* at the bottom to see the complete

list.

Here is another feature to learn. We mentioned earlier that your are looking at the *Details* mode of viewing your files. This is because that is the way it may be set. Let's look at the top row on the right side. You will see near the right end a small icon and a down pointer. When you select the pointer it will give you a context menu with [More options]. This opens a slider menu where you can see that the slider is pointing at *Details* next to that icon. You can change the view by clicking on a different view in the list.

Suppose you are looking at a list of family photos in the *Details* view but want to see thumbnail images of each photo. That's easily done by moving the pointer by clicking on the *Large Icons* near the top. Now you can see your files in picture view with each one showing in a small thumbnail view.

Looking at this graphic you can see an example of this. A variation of this is to leave it in *Details* view. When you select a file, a small thumbnail shows at the bottom left corner. It's small but good for selecting the one you want.

Now let's return to the *Details* setting. With the setting on *Details* now you can see each photo in a much larger view. Put your cursor on the other small icon at the top and it says,

[Show the preview pane]. When you click on it the right edge of the list will move over leaving room for a preview of the selected file.

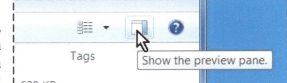

Thus, if you want to see a larger view of each file, click on the small icon at the top right this will open a preview panel to show your selected file as a picture preview. Now select a picture (.jpg) file and it will show a nice view of it larger than the thumbnails. When we copy photos from our camera or Smart phone they are only titled by the number created at the time. This tells us nothing about the picture. Now when you click on one of the files you can see a larger image of it on the right.

If you want to look through many photos it will go faster if you *don't* use the mouse. How then? Click on the first item on the list and use your keyboard down-arrow. Each time you tap it the bar will move to the next item and the image changes to match it. You can see a faint vertical line that separates the photo pane from the listings. This can be moved left or right by setting your cursor on it and when the double arrow appears, drag it to a new location. This will enlarge the preview pane area and the photo in it. Set it where you like it.

This preview works not only for photos but any files. If you have a Family History folder with many written documents, you can look there, set the Preview Pane and go down the list with the down arrow. It will show a part of the file so you can see the title and some of the paragraphs.

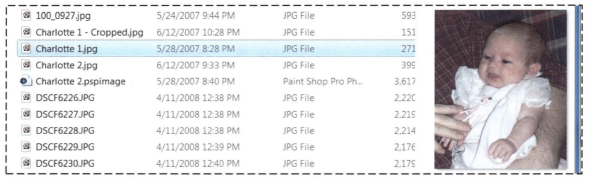

This is an example of a folder with one of my grandchildren shown this way.

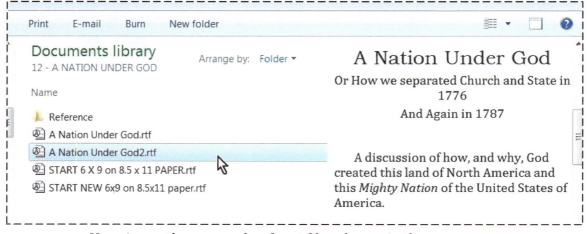

Here is another example of text files shown in the same way.

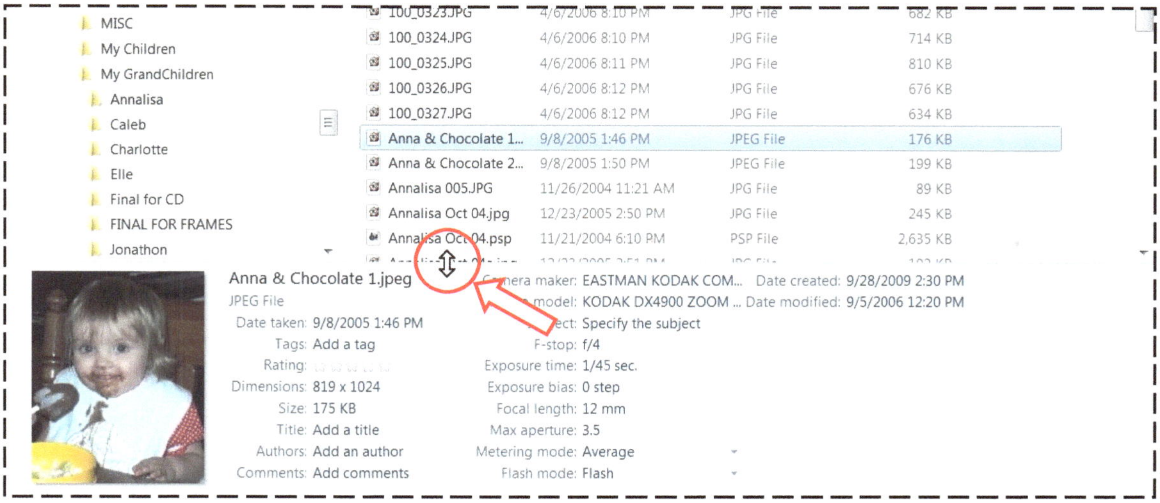

Unfortunately, the Microsoft Office .doc or .docx files won't work in this way. It will only show a note that says "No preview available."

One more trick before we leave this subject. When the View is set to Details there is another way to view the files and to see much more about each one. When you select a file there is an information panel at the bottom. It is light blue and has a faint line running horizontal to separate it from the other two panels.

You can see that an image is shown at the far left and information is in the space next to it. Now if you click on a photo file it will show a thumbnail view of the photo. Want to see it bigger? Place your cursor on the horizontal line and when it changes to a double arrow press down on the mouse button and drag it upward then let go. This will make larger and also the information is more easily seen. This will also be true of any text file. The Word .doc and .docx files will only show a generic image but all the data is shown there.

4. Changing the Column Widths

In the Explorer, you have seen on the right side that information is divided into columns, each with a heading. Depending on the list shown it will be slightly different. If there are folders on that side besides the files, the headings are Name, Date Modified, Type, and Size. If it's only files the headings will be Name, Date, Type, and size. Sometimes you would like to see the columns in a different order. This is simple by just click and hold on the heading and drag it left or right to a new position. You can also extend the column width another way.

If you put your cursor on the faint line that separates one heading for another it will change to a small double arrow. Now carefully double-click there it will expand to the maximum length of the date in that column. This width will vary by the length of the text.

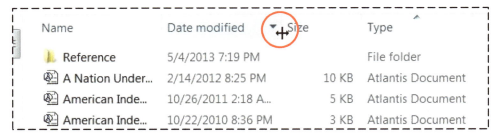

If your list is very long, you can set a filter to show only some of the list. Click on the small down pointer at the end of each heading and will give you some choices. Here is a small window that lets you choose what to see. If you click on the first box it will only show those items in which the first character is a number. Un-check it and check the next one and it will give you an alphabetical list of those letters. Try each of the head-ings and see what they offer as filters of the list.

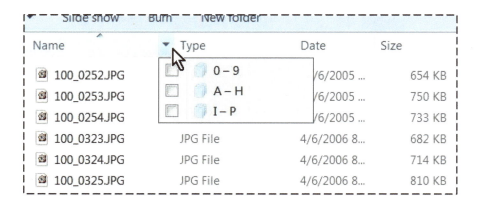

Part 5

Handling the Windows on the Screen

1. Creating You Own Personal Toolbar

You'll remember in Part 1 of this course we learned how to open a small context menu of choices by *right* clicking on different locations. It shows a different menu list depending on where you *right-clicked*. Now, let's *right-click* in an empty space *on the Taskbar* at the bottom and put the cursor on "Toolbars." This brings up the second menu where you will click on "New Toolbar..." item. This will bring up Explorer search window then you can navigate down through your folders to select the one you want.

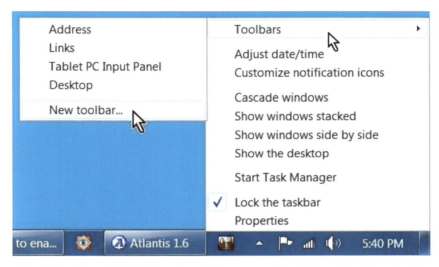

I have chosen the "*My Family*" folder for this example. When I select it then click on *Select Folder* at the bottom, the window is gone and you will see the words "My Family" on the right end of the taskbar with a tiny chevrons symbol pointing to the right.

Click on this symbol on the Taskbar and you will see a list of all the files in that folder. Now if I want to work on one of them I can just select it here and the program that created this file will open. If it's in a lower subfolder then you can rest your cursor on it and its contents will

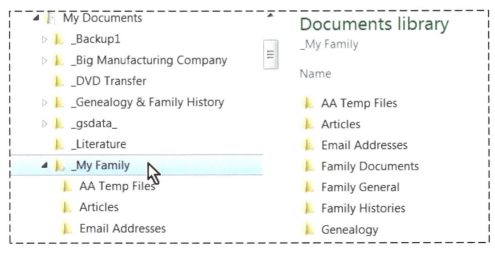

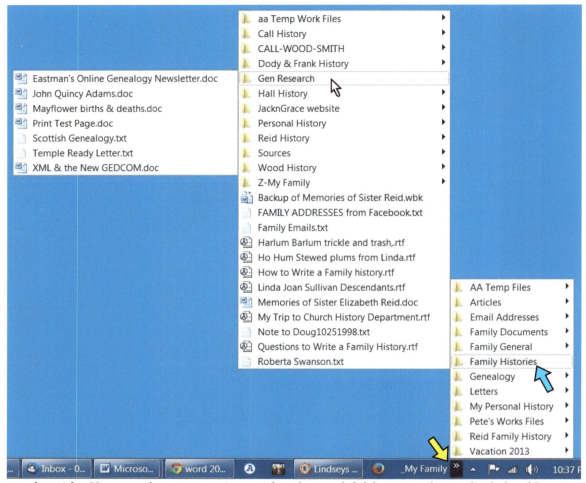

open at the side. You can keep on going with other subfolders until you find the file you want to open. Click on it and the file will open in its own program.

If you want to create a different folder or a second one, you can take these same steps and then search for the other folder and select it. To remove a New Folder from your Toolbar, right-click again on an empty place on the Taskbar and place your cursor on the Toolbars to show the second menu. You will see your toolbar name with a check in front of the name. Just click it and it will terminate.

2. Locking and Unlocking the taskbar

You can do several things with the Taskbar at the bottom but to do anything it first must be *unlocked*. The system has it locked as the default or it may be unlocked already. To see how it is set, right-click on an empty place in the Taskbar and on the small menu look for "Lock the Taskbar." If there is a check mark in front then it is locked. To unlock it click on the check mark to remove it.

You will notice that in the taskbar itself, a divider exists between each area of the taskbar. It looks like a triple row of faint vertical dots. Placing your cursor on the row at the right end, you can drag it left or right to make that space larger or smaller. If you double-click on the

other one, at the left end, it will combine the tabs and compress them to the left. This shows that the personal toolbar I created expands across the space and a third vertical row of dots appears in the Taskbar.

Also, next to this group of dots there is now a small vertical bar with pointers. When you click on either pointer it will show more of the tabs that are not showing to give you access to any of them. Now double-click vertical dots at the left end again and it returns to "normal."

3. Expanding the taskbar

When you are busy working in several programs at once it will make your taskbar become crowded with each program's tab and each tab is compressed. Maybe you have so many that it's hard to read what each one says. One solution to making more space is to unlock the Taskbar then place your cursor on the upper edge of the taskbar until it changes to a double arrow, then carefully *click and hold* the edge and drag the taskbar line upward. You will only need to make it double wide but you could make it much wider. Try it and see.

This will move one row at a time. You can drag it clear to half-way up the screen. Many people like to have two rows to show their many program tabs. Unlocking the Taskbar allows many opportunities to customize the Taskbar your way. Shown here is the double-wide Taskbar. If you want to leave it this way, re-lock the Taskbar.

4. Locking (and unlocking) the Window to the sides of the screen

We are accustomed to seeing the three small boxes in the upper right corner of the screen. They allow us to do three things with the current window: minimize or maximize it, lock and unlock it to the sides, and close the program. To *lock* the program to the sides just click on the center button. Now this fills the entire screen with no other parts showing around the edges.

If we use the center button and *unlock* the current window from the sides of the screen, we can change its size or position. To re-lock it to the edges just click on the middle box again. You can do the same thing by *double-clicking* on the top blue bar of any windows program.

To resize the screen, place your cursor on any of the four sides and when it changes to the double-arrow, drag them in or out then let go. To resize it with a single grip, look at the lower right corner and place your cursor on the tiny dots and drag it any way you want it. Even though it doesn't show a triangle of dots at the other corners, they work the same way. Click on the corner and drag it where you want it.

5. Moving the Window around

It's easy to position any window exactly where you want it. With the window unlocked from the sides, and you have moved the sides to resize it, place your cursor on the top bar then *click and hold* and drag the window where you want it. If it is larger than you would like you can place your cursor on any edge until it changes to a double arrow then *hold and drag* to move that side.

If you wish to move a corner around you can use the small symbols at the lower right corner of <u>every window</u>. Place your cursor on it and wait for it to change and if you are right at the very corner it will be an *angled* double arrow. Hold and drag that corner to modify it's size changing two sides at once. In the small graphic I have laid the PAF window on top of the Word window and you can see the tiny dots in Word but PAF uses the older angled lines. But they work the same.

What is not shown here is that this is doable on *all four corners* of any window. It won't show any symbols—lines or dots—but it works the same nonetheless.

6. Arranging two windows side by side

Often in doing genealogy, besides other work, we need to work in two programs at once and we need to see them side by side. Maybe to *copy and paste* some text from one to the other. Of course, you can use the methods mentioned above to manually resized and position two program screens, but there is a better way.

To see two windows side by side you will need to first clear the screen. Remember from earlier, how you clicked on the tiny rectangle at the right end of the Taskbar and all the programs were cleared off the screen and minimized to the Taskbar. Do that now.

In the example shown, I want to use *FamilySearch* on the right and PAF on the left. To do this I make sure that all the program windows are minimized by clicking the tiny vertical button at the right end of the Taskbar to clear the screen. With the screen cleared I need to select the two windows I want to see together so I will click on the Taskbar to open the two programs I want to see. In this case the PAF program and the FamilySearch window in my browser. Because I want the PAF program on the left I click on it to bring it forward. You can still see the other window behind it.

Now, in the first graphic, I clicked on an empty area of the Taskbar to bring up a context menu and selected "*Show windows side by side*". This will cause both windows to jump to a side-by-side position, fitted perfectly to the screen, with the one previously in front showing on the left.

In the second graphic you will see that to *undo* this, bring up the context menu again and select, "*Undo Show side by side.*" Now they have returned to their original position. This will happen even if one or both of the windows have been locked to the sides of the screen. The "Undo" command will return them to their position before the "side-by-side" command was given.

When viewed side-by-side, you can use the usual copy and paste tools. Many people doing genealogy, with PAF or some other program, like to find their ancestors online and copy them into their personal PAF records. This is a very helpful tool.

If you don't like the arrangement and want to rearrange them, left to right, just repeat the steps but select "*Undo Show side by side.*" to change it back. Then change it the way you like by clicking on the window you want on the left, to bring it forward and reselect "*Show windows*

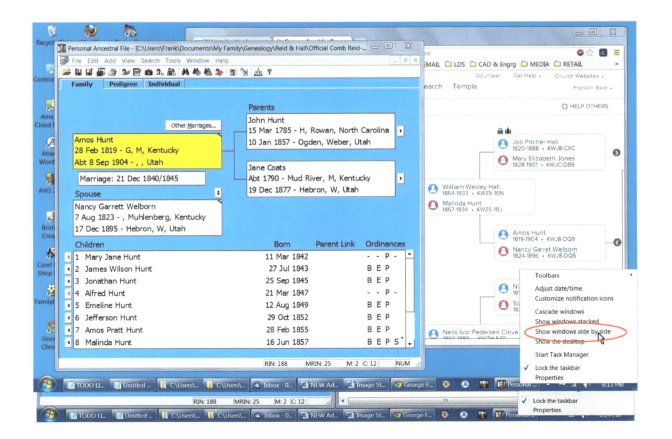

side by side" again.

7. Using the Task Manager

There is a great tool accessible from the Taskbar context menu which can tell you things about your computer. It will also give you the ability to stop a runaway program (it happens!) by ending the task. You can bring it up the same way you have done other things with this menu. Just *right-click* in an empty place on the bottom Taskbar and select *Start Task Manager*.

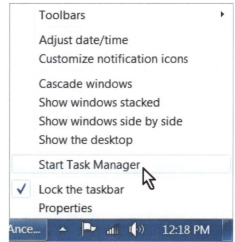

You will see the Windows Task Manager open on your screen. The Processes tab is selected to show all running processes. These are not only programs that you are running but all the little internal programs that run Windows 7. Be careful not to click [End Process] on any of these because then your computer **may stop running!**

But looking at it we can get much helpful information. I have the CPU heading selected so it will arrange the processes in the order of the amount of RAM resource used by each. Notice

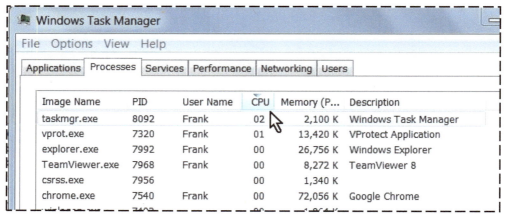

the tiny blue pointer is pointing down, meaning that it is set to show from the largest number to the smallest. If you click it then it will show the reverse. Now if you click on the Applications tab it shows only the programs that you have opened yourself this session.

With the *Applications* tab selected, you can see what programs or "tasks" are currently running on your

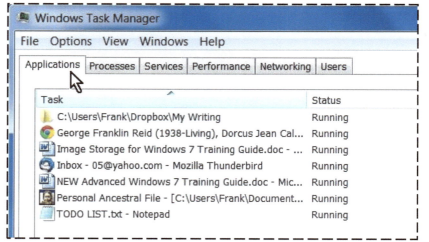

computer. This list should closely match the tabs on the bottom Taskbar. The programs listed all show the Status as "Running." When a program halts or hangs – just stops running – the status will say "Not Responding."

If you need to stop a program and close it down just highlight the name and click on the End Task button. After a moment, it will be removed from this list.

With this tool you can also see the performance of the computer, right now, by clicking on the Performance tab. Notice that this shows a moving progress of the usage of your Central Processing Unit or CPU. This shows what is going on in the RAM. The CPU Usage window shows the current percent of RAM or CPU being used. The CPU Usage History is a running

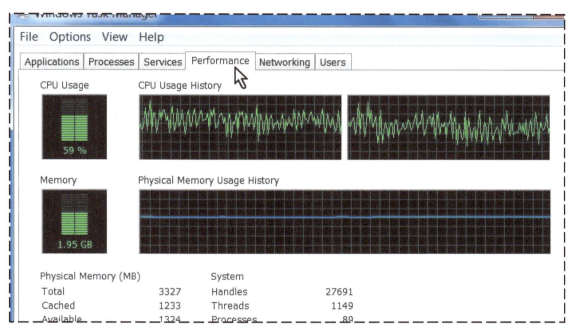

graph of usage.

Below the graphs are the various readings of your system. In the image at the right you can see the total physical memory. At the bottom of the window it shows the running numbers reflected in the CPU Usage above. When you know what is going on inside your computer, it gives you power over it. This tool gives you knowledge and can help you troubleshoot problems when they arise.

Part 6

More Advanced Controls

1. Using the Control Panel

Although Windows 7 has its controls spread out in different locations there is one central place for most of the settings needed to operate all of its functions. This place is called the *Control Panel.* You can find it by clicking on the **Start** button and you find it about mid-way down the blue panel on the right side. If you click on this it will pause, then add another long list to the right. You can also see it in a separate window by *right-clicking* on Control Panel. Then a small window opens. *Click* on *Show on desktop* to set it, then right click on it again and click on Open. The Control Panel will open as a separate window on your desktop.

At your first look at the Control Panel window it seems like an overwhelming amount of icons. Well, that's only because it is! But we will only look at a few. Each one is a unique tool for setting something in the system.

This window should be showing in the *Large icons* view. If not, you can change it by clicking

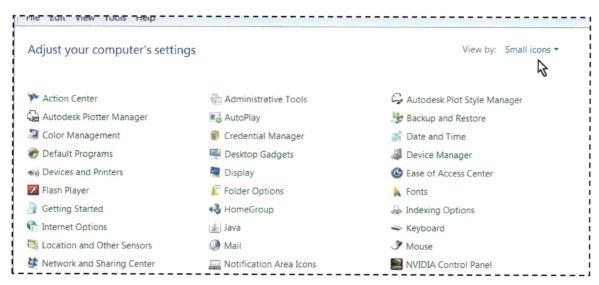

on the words in the upper right corner and change it to *Small icons* or the reverse. This makes the icons smaller and maybe harder to read but also allows more lines on the screen. Drag down the slider on the right side to see others.

Now you can see the many controls you have for your computer. Here you can work on your *Display* monitor, change the *date and time*, the *Sound* system, your *Mouse* settings, and many others. The one called *Programs and Features* we will use later. Like it says at the top, you can "*Adjust your computer's settings.*"

2. Setting the Date and Time

You have done this earlier but you might want to see it here. Let's open one of the icons, one that's easy for us to understand. You will quickly see that these are in ASCII (alphabetical) order from left to right and down the page. In the right column, find the icon called "*Date and Time.*" This is where earlier you set the system clock, calendar, and time zone. Now return to the Control Panel window.

3. Controlling the Display and Mouse

On the Control Panel window, click on the *Display* icon and you will see the same settings we used in **Part 1** to change the background color and to set a photo as our desktop background. Here you can make many display settings which will be seen in all windows. It shows a list on the left of the things you can do such as resolution, color and other things. You've seen this before, you had used the *Personalization* controls to change the window background. At the top of that list it says *Control Panel Home*. Click it to return to the Control Panel window.

Returning to the Control Panel, let's open another icon to change some settings. Find the one called *Mouse* and click on it once. This is the *Mouse Properties* window. With its settings you can change the look function of your mouse. Be aware that others have sat at this same computer and probably set all these settings differently than the default.

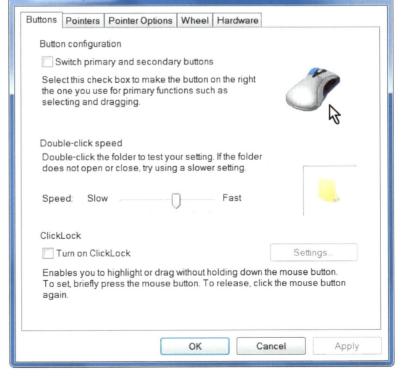

Select the *Buttons* tab and it will let you change the three buttons on your mouse. Yes, three! Left, right, and wheel. A wheel button? If you press down on the wheel it will click giving you another tool to use which will be shown later.

Left-right button setting

Under the Button configuration section there is a small box that can be clicked to Switch primary and secondary buttons. This is how you can set the mouse for *left-handed* use and for people who can't use their right hand on the mouse. While looking at the small graphic of the mouse, and while watching the blue color on the left mouse button, click on the small box. This will cause the mouse color to move to the right button.

Now if you click the tiny box again <u>nothing will happen</u>. Why? Because you switched the buttons! You are still trying to use the left button to *select* with when the mouse has been changed to the *right* button. To change it back use the *right* mouse button to select the box and the check will disappear and the mouse now works normally. Now wasn't that fun?!

Double-Click Speed Setting

You already know that when faced with the computer desktop you can use the icons to start programs by *double-clicking* on them. But sometimes your clicking speed won't do it. You can change the speed needed here. As we get older our hands are not as nimble and quick as they were at a younger age. If you have trouble getting the program icon to open then you probably need to change the *double-click* speed. The second section in this window is for changing the setting. You can test yourself by *double-clicking* on the small graphic at the right. If it opens or closes the folder then it is set right for you. If not, just move the slider to adjust it and try again.

ClickLock Setting

In the third section, ClickLock, there is another box to check if needed. It provides the ability to change how you *click-and-hold* while dragging. Because it's sometimes hard to do, this provides a little help. It is self-explanatory in this section. You can turn on this feature by clicking on the small box. It will open the *Settings* window where you can adjust the time needed to hold the

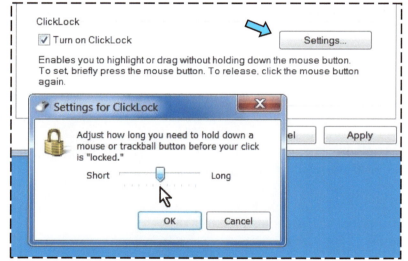

mouse button down. The *Settings* button lets you adjust how long you need to hold down a mouse button before your click is "locked." Then you can click on something to drag by just clicking it *once* then dragging where needed and *click it again* to release the item.

> **<u>Warning:</u>** Be aware that if you leave the box checked it will always be ON regardless of the Short—Long setting. It can be a nuisance if you're not used to it. To change it, return here and click the "Turn on" box to remove the check mark.

Mouse Pointers Choices

Returning to this Mouse Properties window you can see other tabs to make more changes. Click on the *Pointers* tab and in the *Scheme* area you will a place to set your mouse cursor size. Yours is probably set to (None) because that is the default. You can see the example of the setting in the box on the right. Pull down the pointer to see others.

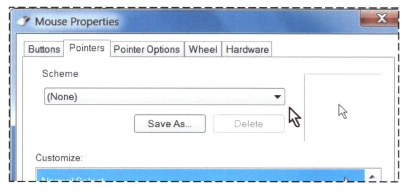

Because I needed a larger mouse pointer to show in this training guide I use the Magnified (system scheme) which is much larger and you can see the difference in the size as shown on the right in my graphic.

Mouse Pointer Options

Now looking at the top of the Mouse Properties window we see other tabs. Click on the *Pointer Options* to see more settings for the mouse cursor. The **Motion** area controls how fast the mouse moves around the screen. To change the speed, move the slider left or right.

Warning: *The change is immediate. If you slide it all the way to Slow it will be snail slow and you will have a hard time getting all the way over to the pointer to move it. Fast is the same, it will jump too far to control it easily.*

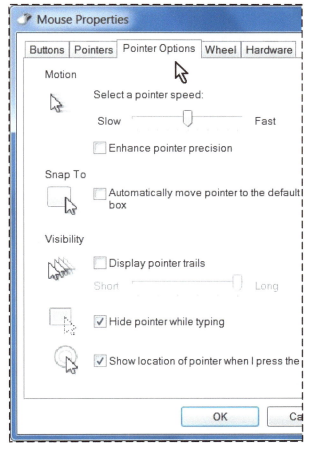

The next area is the **Snap To** setting for use in making changes in programs where you have a default set. As it says, it will *automatically* snap the pointer to the default. Leave this one alone for now.

In the **Visibility** area there are three settings. Some people like to have trailing images on their cursor. This is like a comet trail from the direction you are moving it. Click on it and move the mouse around to see the effect. Click off the check in the box to end it.

The next item is simply a way to turn off the cursor when you start typing in a program so it's not in the way. If you touch the mouse it comes right back.

Finally, the **Show Location** is useful when you can't see where the cursor is. If you click this then hit the Ctrl key on your keyboard it will make a target around it you can easily see. Click to turn off.

Mouse Wheel Settings

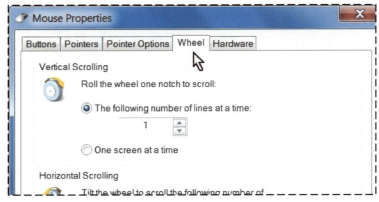

Again at the top of the Mouse Properties window, click on the *Wheel* tab. You already know that if you are in a document and roll the mouse wheel it will scroll the words on the page up or down. The setting in *Vertical Scrolling* lets you control how much it will scroll with each wheel click. You can change it by clicking on the tiny pointers up or down. The default is 3 but you can change it to be slower such as 2 or 1 or even faster with 4 and up to 100 if you wish. If you want your document to move up or down by an entire screen page, just click on the round button below this.

For Horizontal Scrolling it's only useful in very few programs like financial spreadsheet programs where there is a need to move one cell left or right. The next tab is called Hardware and it only shows you the brand and status of the mouse attached to the computer. That is probably enough changes to the mouse for now. Close the Mouse Properties window and return to the Control Panel window.

Your Computer's Information

Now with the Control Panel window open, drag down the slider on the right to see more of the icons. Click on *System* and you will see the window that lets you "**View basic information about your computer.**" Here it shows that my computer is running Windows 7 Professional and that it has an upgrade Service Pack 1 applied.

It also shows the System equipment including the main processor chip and it's clock speed (3.20 GHz), the amount of RAM is 4.00 GB (Giga Bytes), and is a 32-bit operating system. It even tells the brand name of the computer. This is probably more information than you wanted to know at this time. But you may want to come back to these System settings later.

Part 7

More Things to consider

1. Using your Browser

One of the fun things we can do is to use the browser on your computer to "browse" websites on the Internet. If you have a WiFi or other connection you can search for websites. The computer's browser is the window used to search the Internet. The one you are most familiar with is Microsoft *Internet Explorer* which comes with Windows 7. To activate it you need to click on the large Start button or sphere and find it on the list.

This program comes with your Windows operating system and is designed to look <u>outward</u> at the Internet rather than <u>inward</u> at your computer like your *Windows Explorer* we have been using. When you go to your email program you are using your browser. Its method is to use your computer's modem and the Internet Service Provider (ISP) to link your computer onto their website automatically and read your email. From there you can go anywhere else. For instance, if you use gmail, or Yahoo, AOL or MSN or any other email provider, it will take you to that site and show you the email listed for today.

Of all the things you do on the computer you are probably more familiar with the browser and getting your email than anything else. There are several other well-known browsers available. Google Chrome is one, and Mozilla Firefox is another. We won't go into all of them

here as they will require their own training guide. But they all work very much alike although they look different.

To find Internet Explorer click on the Start sphere and click on *All Programs*. Then click on it to open it ready for work. If you are using a different one on your computer it can also be found on the Start list. Each looks much like the others, depending on how you have it set up. They usually have a line of commands at the top and a row of icons for tools. The graphic here is from the top of Internet Explorer.

Next is the browser from Mozilla called Firefox. And finally, there is one here from Google called Chrome. Each of these will use a *search engine*, which is a separate program not part of the browser. The most common search engine is Google which can be found by each of these browsers. Even though Google is the name of the Chrome browser it still functions separately from Google the search engine. At the top there is a long space where you can type in the *Internet address* of where you want to go. It's called a *Uniform Resource Locater* or URL. If you

This is Internet Explorer

type in www.google.com it will take you to the Google website for searching. If you type in www.familysearch.org, it will take you to the LDS Church's genealogy website.

This is Mozilla Firefox

Notice that it requires the exact URL in the form of www followed by a dot, then the name of the site, followed by the type. This type can be .org which means it is a non-profit **org**anization such as a church, a .com which is a **com**mercial site, and .net which can be a **net**work just for information or other use. There are more of these types available when you create a website. Schools and other **edu**cation institutions usually have an .edu type and **gov**ernments have a .gov.

This is Google Chrome

Besides the URL address space there is usually another space for just typing a search word or phrase such as "old cars" or "apple pie" or "pasta recipes" whatever you want to search for. This will bring up a list of many places you can go to for finding your searched item.

2. Using External Storage Devices

USB flash drive.

If you want to store files someplace besides on your hard drive, you can back them up to another device. For many years the standard 3-1/2 inch floppy disk was the most popular. Most newer computers, however, no longer have a floppy drive installed so most people have been using a CD disk or a USB flash drive. Now that the CD/DVD drives are no longer on the newer computers it leaves other possibilities.

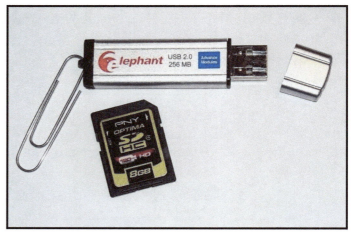

The flash drive is the most common. These small devices are all solid-state which means there are no moving parts. They are very stable and simple to operate. You just plug it into a USB port and the computer recognizes it as another drive on the system. It is called flash because it uses a type of internal memory that can be written to using flash memory technology. It was developed for the memory cards we use in our cameras instead of film and also as a storage in a USB drive. They are about the size of your thumb so some people call them "thumb drives." Others just call them a memory "stick."

In the graphic you can see both a compact flash memory card and an early USB flash drive. These are now used everywhere for storage. If you have one larger than this 256MB drive it will hold much more information such as writings, photos, music, and videos. They make very good external storage drives and can be easily removed and kept elsewhere.

3. Copying to a USB Flash Drive

The easiest way to copy files is to simply use the Explorer, no other software is really needed. Bring up the Explorer and go to the folder where the file is to copy. *Right-click* it and select *Send To*, then the flash drive. The system will copy the file onto the flash drive. If you select the file with a *right-click*, select *Copy*, then put your cursor on a folder on the flash drive and *right-click* and *Paste* it.

The files or group of files will be copied to the flash drive. Then you can check the flash drive by opening it and verify that the files are there. Another way is to highlight the file or files and use your keyboard to type Ctrl+C which will copy the files onto the Clipboard, then highlight where you want them and type Ctrl+V to paste it down.

You can also select and drag the files onto the flash drive. If you use the Ctrl key while doing this you have the option of a Move (meaning copy it and delete the old one) or just a straight copy—your choice.

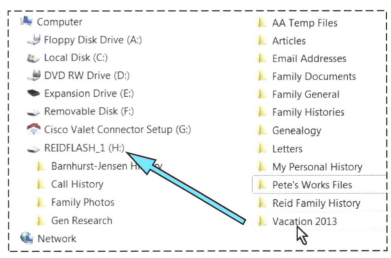

This is the end of the Advance Windows 7 training class, you can use this manual to practice using these same methods. I hope you enjoyed the class and I hope you will have success in your future work with Windows 7. fr